My Bilingual Talking Dictionary

Thai & English

Mantra Lingua

First published in 2005 by Mantra Lingua
Global House, 303 Ballards Lane, London N12 8NP
www.mantralingua.com

This TalkingPEN edition 2012
Text copyright © 2005 Mantra Lingua
Illustrations copyright © 2005 Mantra Lingua
(except pages 4-9, 42-49 Illustrations copyright © 2005 Priscilla Lamont)
Audio copyright © 2009 Mantra Lingua

With thanks to the illustrators:
David Anstey, Dixie Bedford-Stockwell, Louise Daykin,
Alison Hopkins, Richard Johnson, Allan Jones,
Priscilla Lamont, Yokococo

Hear each page of this talking book narrated with the TalkingPEN!
1) To get started touch the arrow button below with the TalkingPEN.
2) To hear the word in English touch the 'E' button at the top of the pages.
3) To hear the word spoken in an English sentence touch the 'S' button at the top of the pages.
4) To hear the language of your choice touch the 'L' button on the top of the pages.
5) Touch the square button below to hear more information about using the Dictionary with the TalkingPEN.

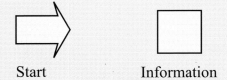

Start   Information

Contents

สารบัญ

Myself

ตา
eyes

ผม
hair

ปาก
mouth

หู
ears

ฟัน
teeth

มือ
hand

นิ้วโป้ง
thumb

ข้อมือ
wrist

นิ้วมือ
fingers

เอว
waist

เท้า
feet

นิ้วเท้า
toes

ความสุข
happy

เสียใจ
sad

โกรธ
angry

อิจฉา
jealous

ตื่นเต้น
excited

ตัวเอง

หน้า
face

ศีรษะ
head

จมูก
nose

คอ
neck

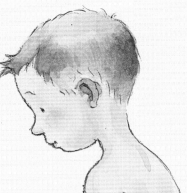

แขน
arm

ไหล่
shoulders

ท้อง
stomach

ข้อศอก
elbow

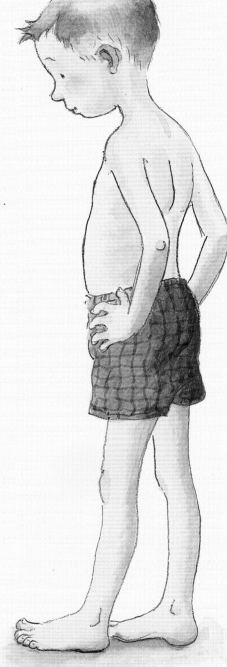

เข่า
knee

หลัง
back

ข้อเท้า
ankle

ขา
leg

ไม่สบาย
sick

หิว
hungry

กลัว
scared

อาย
shy

เหนื่อย
tired

Clothes

เสื้อนอก
coat

ผ้าพันคอ
scarf

เสื้อยืด
t-shirt

ชุดกระโปรง
dress

กระโปรง
skirt

เสื้อไหมพรม
cardigan

ชุดว่ายน้ำ
swimming
costume

ถุงน่อง
tights

กางเกงในหญิง
knickers

รองเท้า
shoes

เสื้อผ้า

 ถุงเท้า
socks

 กางเกงในชาย
underpants

รองเท้าผ้าใบ
trainers

 ถุงมือ
gloves

 หมวก
hat

 เสื้อเชิ้ต
shirt

 เสื้อกันหนาว
jumper

 กางเกงขายาว
trousers

 กางเกงขาสั้น
shorts

 กางเกงว่ายน้ำ
swimming
trunks

Family

ครอบครัว

ย่า
grandmother

ปู่
grandfather

ตา
grandfather

ยาย
grandmother

ป้า/น้า
aunt

พ่อ
father

แม่
mother

ลุง/อา
uncle

พี่ชาย/
น้องชาย
brother

พี่สาว/
น้องสาว
sister

ลูกชาย
son

ลูกสาว
daughter

เด็กทารก
baby

Home

บ้าน

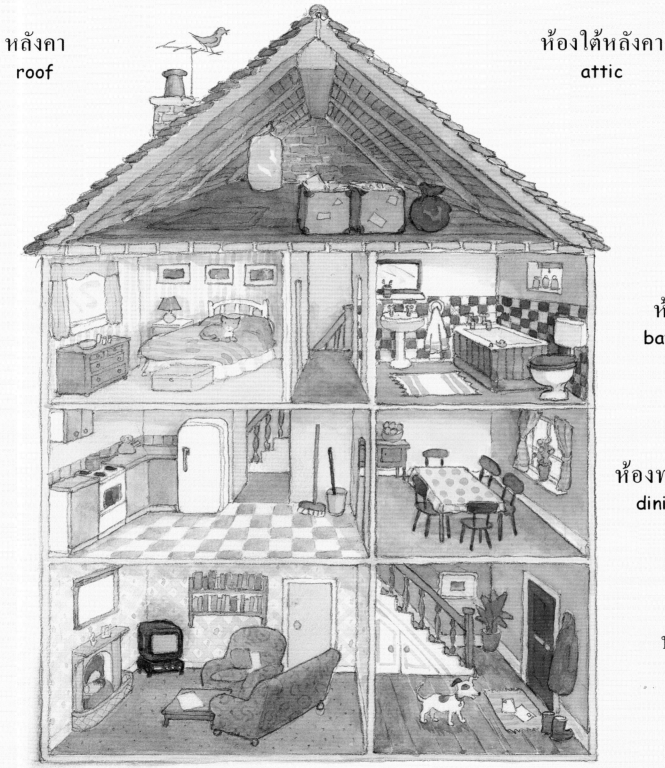

หลังคา
roof

ห้องใต้หลังคา
attic

หน้าต่าง
window

ห้องน้ำ
bathroom

ห้องนอน
bedroom

ห้องทานอาหาร
dining room

ห้องครัว
kitchen

ประตู
door

กำแพง
wall

ห้องนั่งเล่น
lounge/living room

บันได
staircase

ทางเดินเข้าบ้าน
hallway

House and Contents

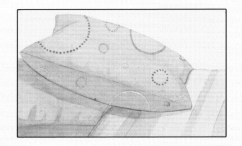

หมอน
pillow

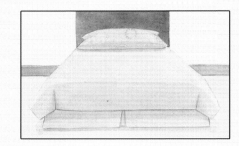

เตียงนอน
bed

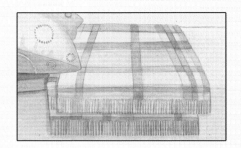

ผ้าห่ม
blanket

ถังขยะ
bin

พัดลม
fan

โคมไฟ
lamp

โทรศัพท์
telephone

เครื่องซักผ้า
washing machine

เครื่องปิ้งขนมปัง
toaster

กาต้มน้ำ
kettle

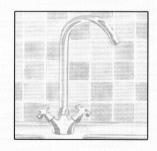

ก๊อกน้ำ
tap

ตู้เย็น
fridge

ภาชนะหุงต้ม
cooker

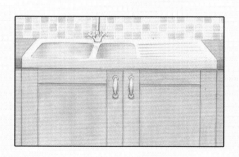

อ่างล้างจาน
sink

บ้านและของใช้ในบ้าน

เครื่องทำความร้อน
radiator

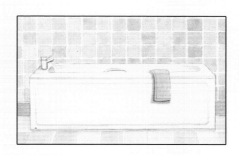

อ่างอาบน้ำ
bath

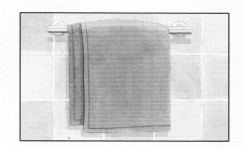

ผ้าขนหนู
towel

กระจกเงา
mirror

ห้องน้ำ
toilet

กระดาษชำระ
toilet roll

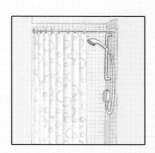

ฝักบัวอาบน้ำ
shower

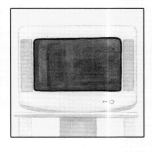

โทรทัศน์
television

วิทยุ
radio

ผ้าม่าน
curtains

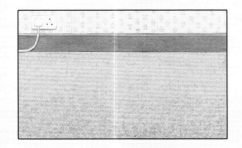

ตู้
cupboard

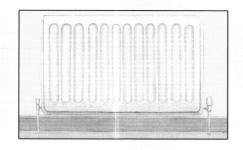

พรม
carpet

เก้าอี้โซฟา
sofa

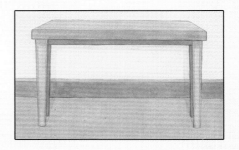

โต๊ะ
table

Fruit

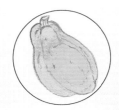
กล้วย
banana

มะละกอ
papaya

ลูกแพร์
pear

แตง
melon

ลูกพลัม
plum

มะนาว
lemon

เชอรี่
cherries

สตรอเบอรี่
strawberries

ผลไม้

องุ่น
grapes

สับปะรด
pineapple

มะม่วง
mango

ส้ม
orange

ลูกพีช
peach

แอปเปิ้ล
apple

ลิ้นจี่
lychees

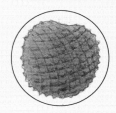

ผลทับทิม
pomegranate

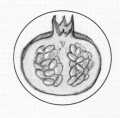

Vegetables

 หัวหอม
onion

 ดอกกะหล่ำ
cauliflower

 มันฝรั่ง
potato

 ข้าวโพด
sweetcorn

 เห็ด
mushroom

 มะเขือเทศ
tomato

 ถั่วฝักยาว
beans

 หัวไชเท้า
radish

กระเทียม
garlic

ฟักทอง
pumpkin/squash

แตงกวา
cucumber

บร็อคโคลี่
broccoli
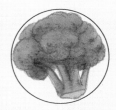

พริกไทย
pepper/capsicum

แครอท
carrot

ผักกาด
lettuce

ถั่วลันเตา
peas
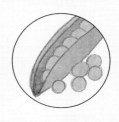

Food and Drink

ขนมปัง
bread

เนย
butter

แยม
jam

แซนวิช
sandwich

น้ำตาล
sugar

น้ำผึ้ง
honey

ธัญพืช
cereal

นม
milk

ก๋วยเตี๋ยว
noodles

ข้าว
rice

สปาเก็ตตี้
spaghetti

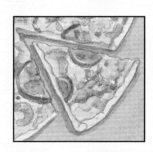

พิชซ่า
pizza

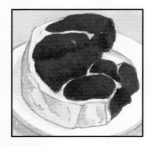

เนื้อ
meat

ปลา
fish

ไข่
egg

เนยแข็ง
cheese

ช็อกโกแลต
chocolate

ขนมหวาน
sweets

ขนมเค้ก
cake

ขนมพุดดิ้ง
pudding

นมเปรี้ยว
yoghurt

ไอศครีม
ice cream

ขนมปังกรอบ
biscuit

ขนมขบเคี้ยว
crisps

มันฝรั่ง
chips

ซอสมะเขือเทศ
ketchup

มัสตาร์ด
mustard

น้ำแกง
soup

น้ำผลไม้
fruit juice

น้ำแร่
mineral water

เกลือ
salt

พริกไทย
pepper

Meal Time

มีด
knife

ส้อม
fork

ช้อน
spoon

ตะเกียบ
chopsticks

เหยือก
mug

ถ้วย
cup

แก้ว
glass

เวลารับประทานอาหาร

จาน
plate

ชาม
bowl

กระทะใส่ซอส
saucepan

หม้อ
wok

กระทะ
frying pan

กระติกเก็บน้ำร้อน
flask

กล่องอาหาร
lunchbox

Town

 ซูเปอร์มาร์เก็ต
supermarket

 ที่จอดรถ
car park

 ศูนย์กีฬา
sports centre

 ห้องสมุด
library

 สถานีตำรวจ
police station

 สถานีรถไฟ
train station

 สถานีดับเพลิง
fire station

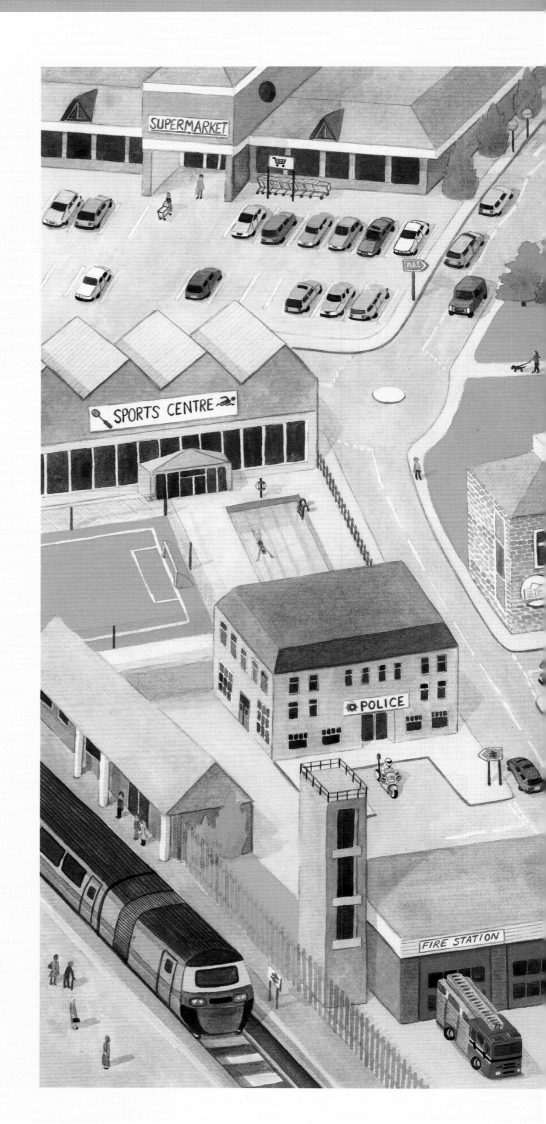

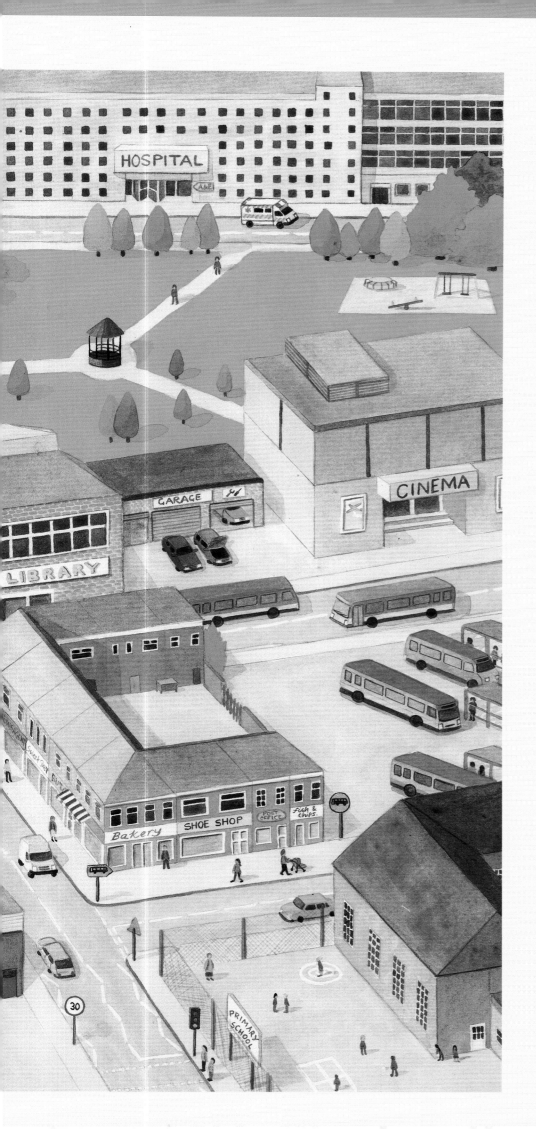

โรงพยาบาล
hospital

สวนสาธารณะ
park

โรงภาพยนตร์
cinema

โรงจอดรถ
garage

สถานีรถโดยสาร
bus station

ร้านค้า
shops/stores

โรงเรียน
school

High Street

ร้านอาหาร
restaurant

ร้านดอกไม้
florist

แผงขายหนังสือพิมพ์
newspaper stand

ร้านหนังสือ
book shop

ร้านขายเนื้อ
butcher

ไปรษณีย์
post office

ร้านขายปลา
fishmonger

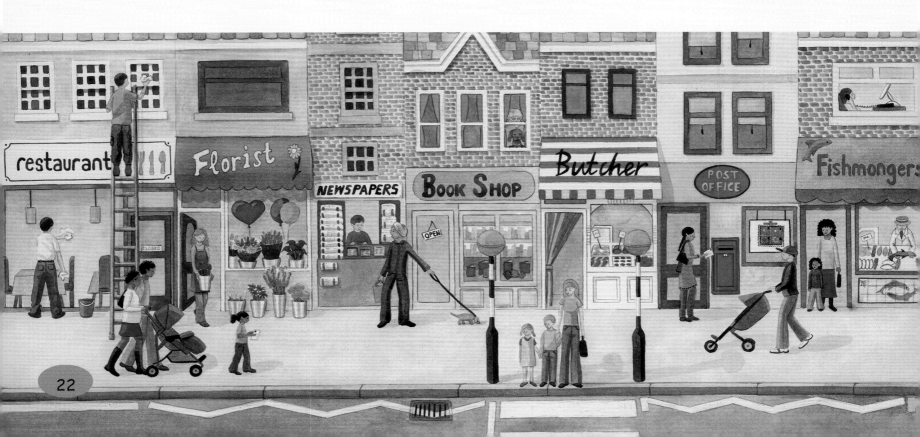

ร้านผักและผลไม้สด
greengrocer

ร้านขายยา
chemist

ร้านขนมปัง
bakery

ธนาคาร
bank

ร้านของเล่น
toyshop

ร้านกาแฟ
coffee shop

ร้านตัดผม
hairdressers

Road Safety

ถนน
road

สัญญาณไฟจราจร
traffic light

ไฟแดงห้ามคนข้ามถนน
red man

ไฟเขียวคนข้ามถนน
green man

แสงสว่าง
lights

สิ่งสะท้องแสง
reflector

หมวกกันน๊อค
cycle helmet

ทางม้าลาย
pedestrian crossing

ไป
go

หยุด
stop

มองดู
look

ฟัง
listen

ทางข้ามถนนสำหรับเด็ก
children crossing

เจ้าหน้าที่จราจร
หน้าโรงเรียน
school crossing
patrol officer

เข็มขัดนิรภัย
seat belt

ทางเท้า
pavement

Transport

เครื่องบิน
aeroplane

รถบรรทุก
lorry/truck

รถยนต์
car

รถทัวร์
coach

เรือ
boat

รถจักรยาน
bicycle

รถไฟ
train

รถจักรยานยนต์
motorbike

เฮลิคอปเตอร์
helicopter

รถประจำทาง
bus

รถราง
tram

รถคาราวาน
caravan

เรือใหญ่
ship

รถลาก
rickshaw

Farm Animals

 นก
bird

 ม้า
horse

 เป็ด
duck

 แมว
cat

 แพะ
goat

 กระต่าย
rabbit

 สุนัขจิ้งจอก
fox

ฟาร์มสัตว์

วัว
cow

สุนัข
dog

แกะ
sheep

หนู
mouse

แม่ไก่
hen

ลา
donkey

ห่าน
goose

Wild Animals

ลิง
monkey

ช้าง
elephant

งู
snake

ม้าลาย
zebra

สิงโต
lion

ฮิปโป
hippopotamus

ปลาโลมา
dolphin

ปลาวาฬ
whale

สัตว์ป่า

หมีแพนด้า
panda bear

ยีราฟ
giraffe

อูฐ
camel

เสือ
tiger

หมี
bear

นกเพนกวิน
penguin

จระเข้
crocodile

ปลาฉลาม
shark

Seaside

ทะเล
sea

คลื่น
waves

ชายหาด
beach

คนดูแลความปลอดภัย
lifeguard

ครีมกันแดด
sun lotion

เปลือกหอย
shells

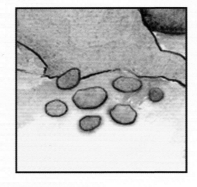

ก้อนกรวด
pebbles

สาหร่ายทะเล
seaweed

สระน้ำที่มีก้อนหิน
ล้อมรอบ
rock pool

ปู
crab

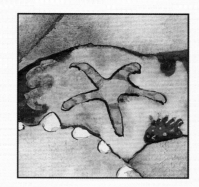

ปลาดาว
starfish

เก้าอี้พับได้
deckchair

ทราย
sand

ปราสาททราย
sandcastle

ถังน้ำ
bucket

พลั่ว
spade

Playground

แกว่ง
swing

ม้าหมุน
roundabout

ไม้กระดก
seesaw

สนามทราย
sandpit

อุโมงค์
tunnel

ข้างใน
in

ข้างนอก
out

กระโดด
skip

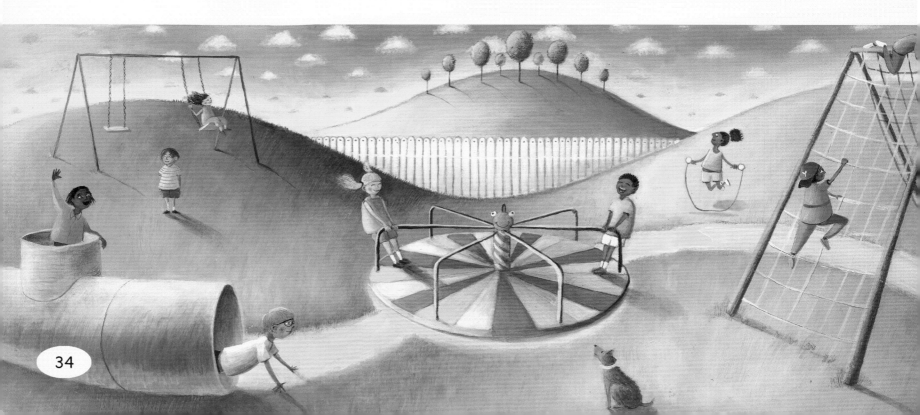

กระดานไต่เชือก
climbing frame

ขึ้น
up

ลื่น
slide

ลง
down

ข้าม
over

ใต้
under

ข้างหน้า
in front

ข้างหลัง
behind

The Classroom

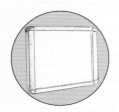

กระดาน
white board

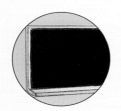

กระดานดำ
chalk board

โต๊ะเขียนหนังสือ
desk

เก้าอี้
chair

ปฏิทิน
calendar

เครื่องอัดเทป
tape recorder

เทป
cassette tape

เครื่องคิดเลข
calculator

ห้องเรียน

ครู
teacher

หนังสือ
books

กระดาษ
paper
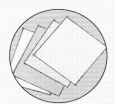

สี
paint

แปรงทาสี
paintbrush

กรรไกร
scissors

กาว
glue

สก็อตเทป
sticky tape

School Bag

 สมุดสำหรับเขียน
writing book

 สมุดเลข
maths book

 แฟ้ม
folder

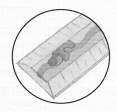 ไม้บรรทัด
ruler

 ไม้โปร
protractor

 ดินสอ
pencil

 กบเหลาดินสอ
pencil sharpener

หนังสือสำหรับอ่าน
reading book

ดินสอเทียน
crayon

เชือก
string

เงิน
money

วงเวียน
compass

ยางลบ
rubber/eraser

ปากกาเมจิก
felt tip pen

Computers

เครื่องสแกนรูปภาพ
scanner

เครื่องคอมพิวเตอร์
computer

จอคอมพิวเตอร์
monitor

แป้นพิมพ์
keyboard

เม้าส์
mouse

แผ่นรองเม้าส์
mouse mat

เครื่องพิมพ์
printer

จอ
screen

อินเตอร์เน็ต
internet

จดหมายอิเล็คทรอนิกส์
email

แผ่นซีดี
cd disc

แผ่นดิสต์
floppy disc

Dressing Up

นักบิน
astronaut

ตำรวจ
police person

สัตวแพทย์
vet

นักดับเพลิง
firefighter

จิตรกร
artist

เจ้าของร้าน
shop keeper

นักขี่ม้า
jockey

โคบาล
cowboy

คนครัว
chef

นางพยาบาล
nurse

ช่างเครื่องยนต์
mechanic

คนขับรถไฟ
train driver

นักเต้นบัลเล่ต์
ballet dancer

ดารานักร้องที่มีชื่อเสียง
pop star

ตัวตลก
clown

โจรสลัด
pirate

พ่อมด
wizard

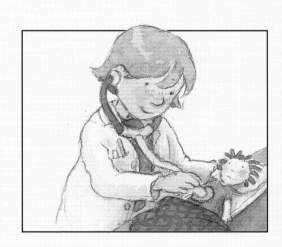

หมอ
doctor

Toys and Games

ลูกโป่ง
balloon

ลูกปัด
beads

เกมที่มีกระดาน
board game

ตุ๊กตา
doll

บ้านตุ๊กตา
doll's house

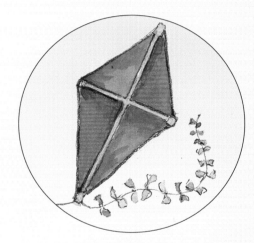

ว่าว
kite

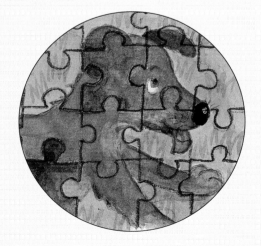

ตัวต่อ
puzzle

กระโดดเชือก
skipping rope

ลูกข่าง
spinning top

เกมต่อตึก
building blocks

หมากรุก
chess

ลูกเต๋า
dice

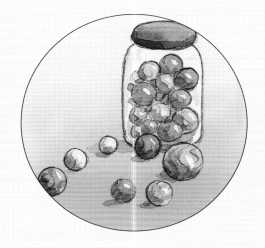

ลูกแก้ว
marbles

ไพ่
playing cards

หุ่นเชิด
puppet

ตุ๊กตาหมีเท็ดดี้
teddy bear

ชุดรถไฟเด็กเล่น
train set

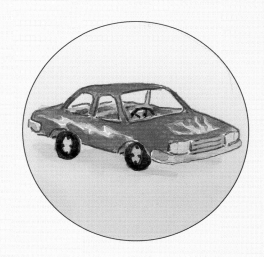

รถเด็กเล่น
toy car

Sport

บาสเก็ตบอล
basketball

ลูกบอล
ball

กีฬาคริกเก็ต
cricket

แบดมินตัน
badminton

ว่ายน้ำ
swimming

รองเท้าสเกต
roller skates

ไม้ตีลูกเทนนิส
racquet

รองเท้าสเกตน้ำแข็ง
ice skates

เทนนิส
tennis

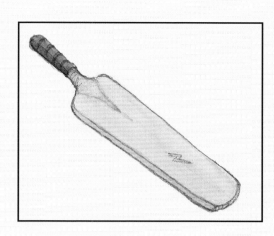

ไม้ตีลูกบอล
bat

เนตบอล
netball

ฟุตบอล
football

ปั่นจักรยาน
cycling

รักบี้
rugby

กระดานสเกตที่มีลูกล้ออยู่ข้างใต้
skateboard

ฮอกกี้
hockey

Music

กลอง
drum

กลองอินเดีย
tabla

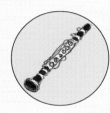
ปี่ลิ้นเดียว
clarinet

ขลุ่ย
flute

พิณตั้ง
harp

คีย์บอร์ด
keyboard

กีต้าร์
guitar

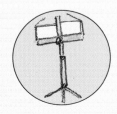
ที่วางแผ่น
โน๊ตดนตรี
music stand

เครื่องดนตรี
สามเหลี่ยม
musical triangle

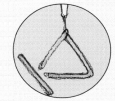

แตร
trumpet

ลูกแซค
maracas

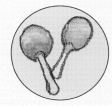

กลองแอฟริกัน
gan gan

เปียโน
piano

เครื่องบันทึกเสียง
recorder

ไวโอลิน
violin

เครื่องดนตรี
ประเภทระนาด
xylophone

Space

ดวงอาทิตย์
sun

ดาวพุธ
Mercury

ดาวศุกร์
Venus

โลก
Earth

ดวงจันทร์
moon

ยานอวกาศ
spaceship

ดาวตก
shooting star

จรวด
rocket

ดาวอังคาร
Mars

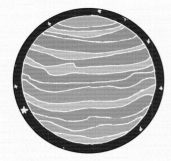

ดาวพฤหัส
Jupiter

ดาวเสาร์
Saturn

ดาวยูเรนัส
Uranus

ดาวหาง
comet

ดวงดาว
stars

ดาวเนปจูน
Neptune

ดาวพลูโต
Pluto

Weather

แดดออก
sunny

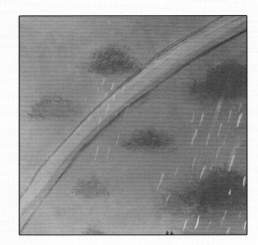

สายรุ้ง
rainbow

ฝนตก
rainy

ฟ้าร้อง
thunder

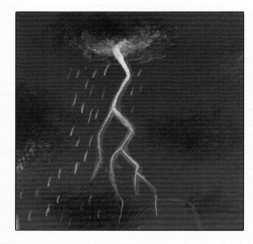

ฟ้าแลบ
lightning

มีพายุ
stormy

ลมแรง
windy

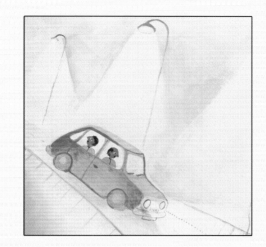

มีหมอก
foggy

หิมะตก
snowy

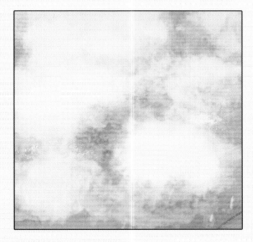

มีเมฆ
cloudy

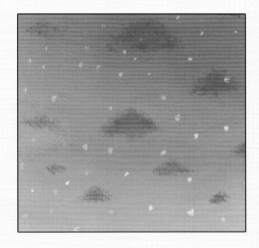

ลูกเห็บ
hail

อากาศหนาวเย็น
icy

Months of the Year

เดือน

 มกราคม
January

 กุมภาพันธ์
February

 มีนาคม
March

 เมษายน
April

 พฤษภาคม
May

 มิถุนายน
June

 กรกฎาคม
July

 สิงหาคม
August

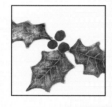 กันยายน
September

 ตุลาคม
October

 พฤศจิกายน
November

 ธันวาคม
December

Seasons

ฤดู

ฤดูใบไม้ผลิ
Spring

ฤดูร้อน
Summer

ฤดูใบไม้ร่วง
Autumn/Fall

ฤดูหนาว
Winter

ฤดูฝน
Monsoon

Days of the Week

วัน

วันจันทร์
Monday

วันอังคาร
Tuesday

วันพุธ
Wednesday

วันพฤหัสบดี
Thursday

วันศุกร์
Friday

วันเสาร์
Saturday

วันอาทิตย์
Sunday

Telling the Time

บอกเวลา

นาฬิกา
clock

วัน
day

เวลากลางคืน
night

เวลาเช้า
morning

เวลาเย็น
evening

นาฬิกาข้อมือ
watch

ผ่านมา 15
นาทีแล้ว
quarter past

ผ่านมาครึ่งชั่ว
โมงแล้ว
half past

อีก 15 นาทีถึง
quarter to

Colours สี

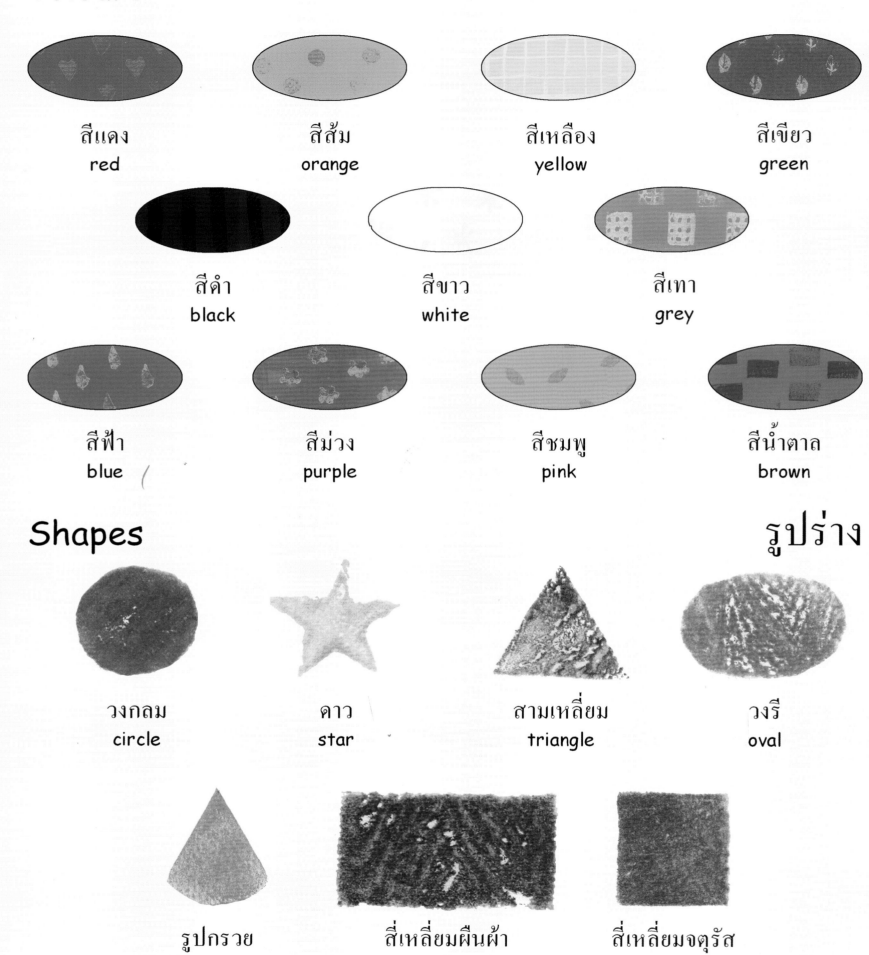

สีแดง
red

สีส้ม
orange

สีเหลือง
yellow

สีเขียว
green

สีดำ
black

สีขาว
white

สีเทา
grey

สีฟ้า
blue

สีม่วง
purple

สีชมพู
pink

สีน้ำตาล
brown

Shapes รูปร่าง

วงกลม
circle

ดาว
star

สามเหลี่ยม
triangle

วงรี
oval

รูปกรวย
cone

สี่เหลี่ยมผืนผ้า
rectangle

สี่เหลี่ยมจตุรัส
square

Numbers 1-20

	1	หนึ่ง one		11	สิบเอ็ด eleven
	2	สอง two		12	สิบสอง twelve
	3	สาม three		13	สิบสาม thirteen
	4	สี่ four		14	สิบสี่ fourteen
	5	ห้า five		15	สิบห้า fifteen
	6	หก six		16	สิบหก sixteen
	7	เจ็ด seven		17	สิบเจ็ด seventeen
	8	แปด eight		18	สิบแปด eighteen
	9	เก้า nine		19	สิบเก้า nineteen
	10	สิบ ten		20	ยี่สิบ twenty

Opposites

เร็ว	ช้า	เปิด	ปิด
fast	slow	open	closed

ใหญ่	เล็ก	เปียก	แห้ง
large	small	wet	dry

ร้อน	เย็น	หวาน	เปรี้ยว
hot	cold	sweet	sour

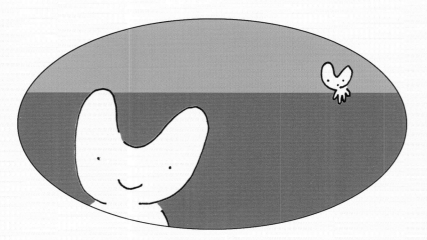

ใกล้
near

ไกล
far

ซ้าย
left

ขวา
right

หน้า
front

หลัง
back

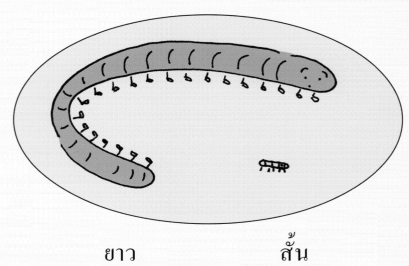

ยาว
long

สั้น
short

หนัก
heavy

เบา
light

ว่างเปล่า
empty

เต็ม
full

Index

Search for a word by picture or by the English word

60

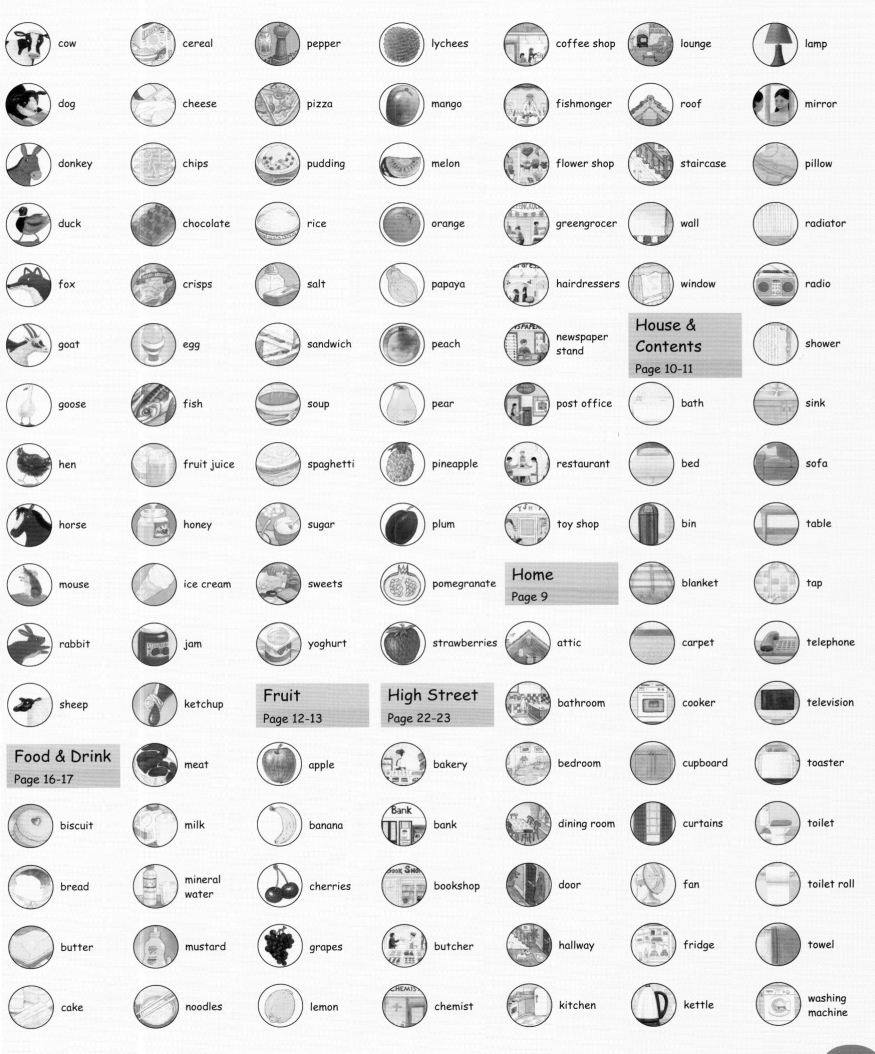

cow	cereal	pepper	lychees	coffee shop	lounge	lamp
dog	cheese	pizza	mango	fishmonger	roof	mirror
donkey	chips	pudding	melon	flower shop	staircase	pillow
duck	chocolate	rice	orange	greengrocer	wall	radiator
fox	crisps	salt	papaya	hairdressers	window	radio
goat	egg	sandwich	peach	newspaper stand	**House & Contents** Page 10-11	shower
goose	fish	soup	pear	post office	bath	sink
hen	fruit juice	spaghetti	pineapple	restaurant	bed	sofa
horse	honey	sugar	plum	toy shop	bin	table
mouse	ice cream	sweets	pomegranate	**Home** Page 9	blanket	tap
rabbit	jam	yoghurt	strawberries	attic	carpet	telephone
sheep	ketchup	**Fruit** Page 12-13	**High Street** Page 22-23	bathroom	cooker	television
Food & Drink Page 16-17	meat	apple	bakery	bedroom	cupboard	toaster
biscuit	milk	banana	bank	dining room	curtains	toilet
bread	mineral water	cherries	bookshop	door	fan	toilet roll
butter	mustard	grapes	butcher	hallway	fridge	towel
cake	noodles	lemon	chemist	kitchen	kettle	washing machine

Meal Time
Page 18-19

bowl
chopsticks
cup
flask
fork
frying pan
glass
knife
lunchbox
mug
plate
saucepan
spoon
wok

Months of the Year
Page 54

January
February
March
April
May
June
July
August
September
October
November
December

Music
Page 48-49

clarinet
drum
flute
gan gan
guitar
harp
keyboard
maracas
musical triangle
music stand
piano
recorder
tabla
trumpet
violin
xylophone

Myself
Page 4-5

angry
ankle
arm
back
ears
elbow
excited
eyes
face
feet
fingers
hair
hand
happy
head
hungry
jealous
knee
leg
mouth
neck
nose
sad
scared
shoulders
shy
sick
stomach
teeth
thumb
tired
toes
waist
wrist

Numbers 1-20
Page 57

one
two
three
four
five
six
seven
eight
nine
ten
eleven
twelve
thirteen
fourteen
fifteen
sixteen
seventeen
eighteen
nineteen
twenty

Opposites
Page 58-59

back
closed
cold
dry
empty
far
fast
front
full
heavy
hot
large
left
light
long
near

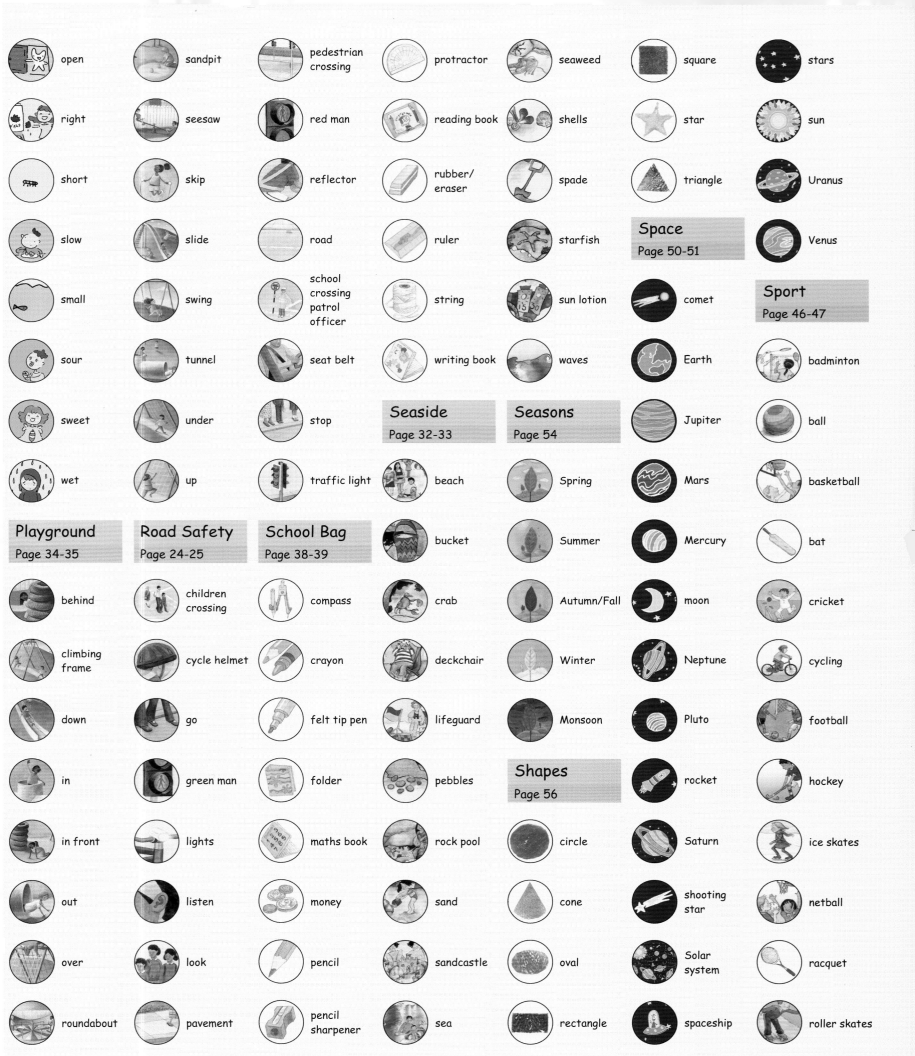

open

right

short

slow

small

sour

sweet

wet

sandpit

seesaw

skip

slide

swing

tunnel

under

up

pedestrian crossing

red man

reflector

road

school crossing patrol officer

seat belt

stop

traffic light

protractor

reading book

rubber/eraser

ruler

string

writing book

seaweed

shells

spade

starfish

sun lotion

waves

square

star

triangle

Space
Page 50-51

comet

Earth

Jupiter

stars

sun

Uranus

Venus

Sport
Page 46-47

badminton

ball

Playground
Page 34-35

behind

climbing frame

down

in

in front

out

over

roundabout

Road Safety
Page 24-25

children crossing

cycle helmet

go

green man

lights

listen

look

pavement

School Bag
Page 38-39

compass

crayon

felt tip pen

folder

maths book

money

pencil

pencil sharpener

Seaside
Page 32-33

beach

bucket

crab

deckchair

lifeguard

pebbles

rock pool

sand

sandcastle

sea

Seasons
Page 54

Spring

Summer

Autumn/Fall

Winter

Monsoon

Shapes
Page 56

circle

cone

oval

rectangle

Mars

Mercury

moon

Neptune

Pluto

rocket

Saturn

shooting star

Solar system

spaceship

basketball

bat

cricket

cycling

football

hockey

ice skates

netball

racquet

roller skates

63

 rugby

 cinema

 chess

 boat

 cucumber

 foggy

 crocodile

 skateboard

 fire station

 dice

 bus

 garlic

 hail

 dolphin

 swimming

 garage

 doll

 car

 lettuce

 icy

 elephant

 tennis

 hospital

 doll's house

 caravan

 mushroom

 lightning

 giraffe

Telling the Time
Page 55

 library

 kite

 coach

 onion

 rainbow

 hippopotamus

 clock

 park

 marbles

 helicopter

 peas

 rainy

 lion

 day

 police station

 playing cards

 lorry/truck

 pepper/ capsicum

 snowy

 monkey

 evening

 school

 puppet

 motorbike

 potato

 stormy

 panda bear

 half past

 shops/ stores

 puzzle

 rickshaw

 pumpkin/ squash

 sunny

 penguin

 morning

 sports centre

 skipping rope

 ship

 radish

thunder

shark

night

 supermarket

spinning top

train

sweetcorn

windy

snake

 quarter past

 train station

 teddy bear

tram

tomato

Wild Animals
Page 30-31

 tiger

 quarter to

Toys and Games
Page 44-45

train set

Vegetables
Page 14-15

Weather
Page 52-53

 bear

whale

 watch

 balloon

toy car

beans

cloudy

camel

zebra

Town
Page 20-21

beads

Transport
Page 26-27

broccoli

bus station

board game

aeroplane

carrot

car park

building blocks

bicycle

 cauliflower